I was good to myself:

Ways I handled conflicts:

Boundaries I set:

Problem areas I noticed:

I am grateful for

Reflections

I was good to myself:

Boundaries I set:

I am grateful for

Date

Ways I handled conflicts:

Problem areas I noticed:

Reflections

I was good to myself:

Date

Ways I handled conflicts:

Boundaries I set:

Problem areas I noticed:

I am grateful for

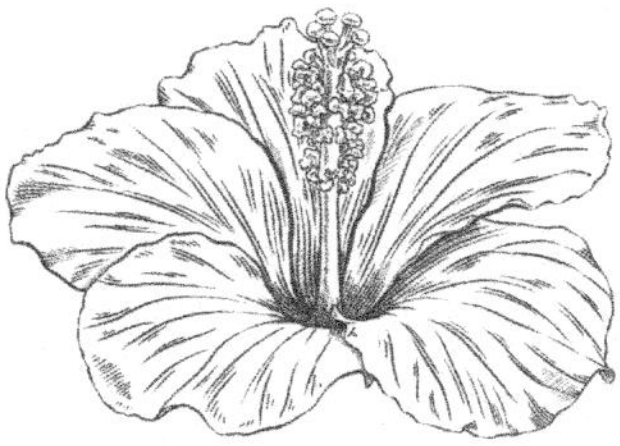

Reflections

I was good to myself:

Date

Ways I handled conflicts:

Boundaries I set:

Problem areas I noticed:

I am grateful for

Reflections

I was good to myself:

Date

Ways I handled conflicts:

Boundaries I set:

Problem areas I noticed:

I am grateful for

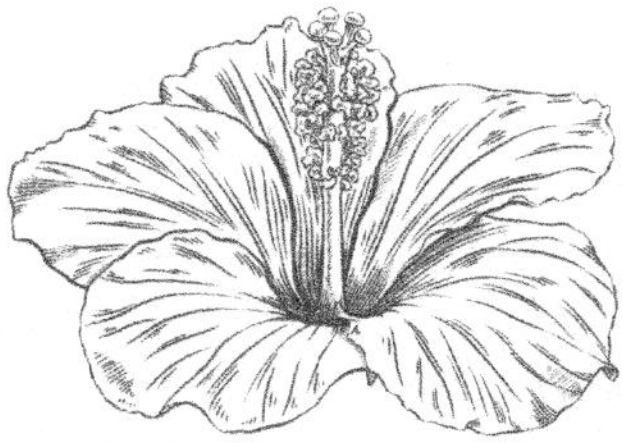

Reflections

I was good to myself:

Date

Ways I handled conflicts:

Boundaries I set:

Problem areas I noticed:

I am grateful for

Reflections

I was good to myself:

Date

Ways I handled conflicts:

Boundaries I set:

Problem areas I noticed:

I am grateful for

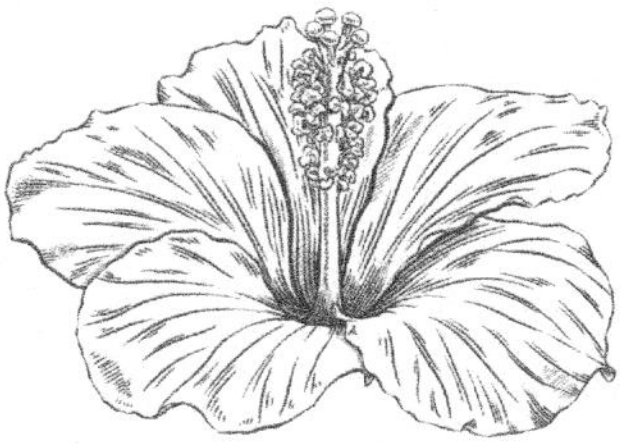

Reflections

I was good to myself:

Date

Ways I handled conflicts:

Boundaries I set:

Problem areas I noticed:

I am grateful for

Reflections

I was good to myself:

Date

Ways I handled conflicts:

Boundaries I set:

Problem areas I noticed:

I am grateful for

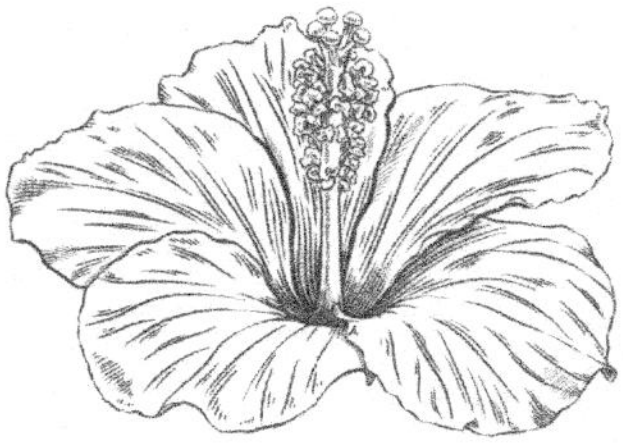

Reflections

Date

I was good to myself:

Ways I handled conflicts:

Boundaries I set:

Problem areas I noticed:

I am grateful for

Reflections

I was good to myself:

Date

Ways I handled conflicts:

Boundaries I set:

Problem areas I noticed:

I am grateful for

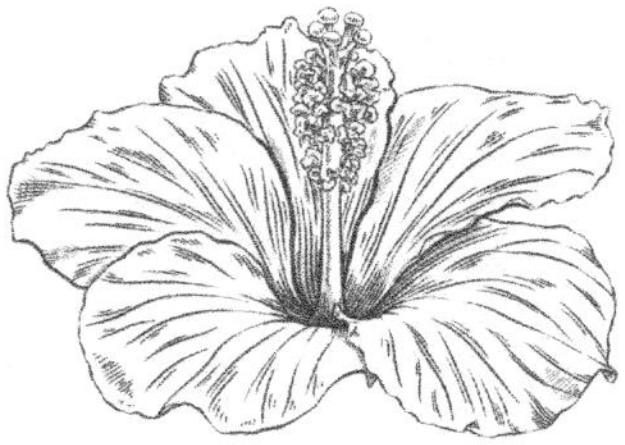

Reflections

I was good to myself:

Date

Ways I handled conflicts:

Boundaries I set:

Problem areas I noticed:

I am grateful for

Reflections

I was good to myself:

Date

Ways I handled conflicts:

Boundaries I set:

Problem areas I noticed:

I am grateful for

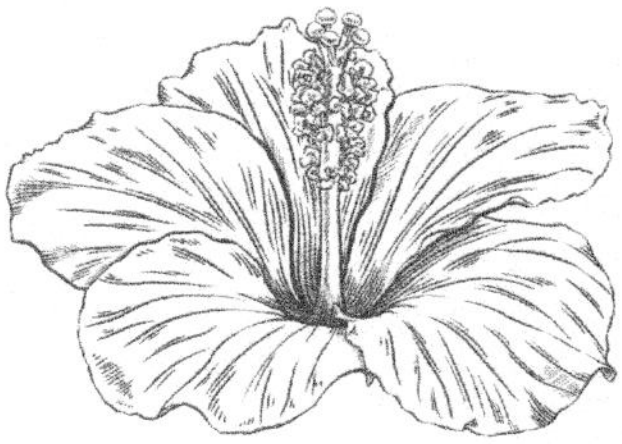

Reflections

I was good to myself:

Boundaries I set:

I am grateful for

Date

Ways I handled conflicts:

Problem areas I noticed:

Reflections

I was good to myself:

Date

Ways I handled conflicts:

Boundaries I set:

Problem areas I noticed:

I am grateful for

Reflections

I was good to myself:

Date

Ways I handled conflicts:

Boundaries I set:

Problem areas I noticed:

I am grateful for

Reflections

I was good to myself:

Date

Ways I handled conflicts:

Boundaries I set:

Problem areas I noticed:

I am grateful for

Reflections

I was good to myself:

Date

Ways I handled conflicts:

Boundaries I set:

Problem areas I noticed:

I am grateful for

Reflections

I was good to myself:

Date

Ways I handled conflicts:

Boundaries I set:

Problem areas I noticed:

I am grateful for

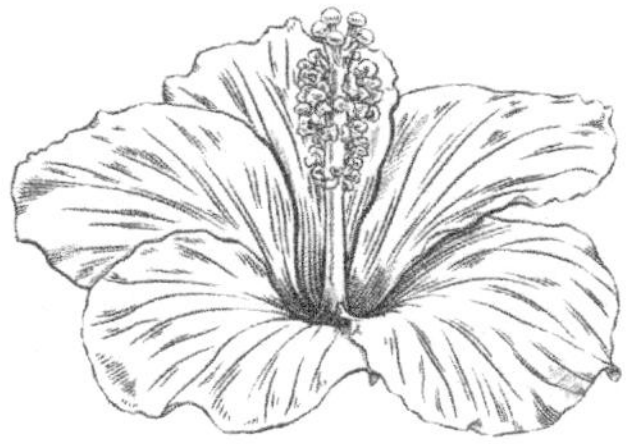

Reflections

I was good to myself:

Date

Ways I handled conflicts:

Boundaries I set:

Problem areas I noticed:

I am grateful for

Reflections

I was good to myself:

Date

Ways I handled conflicts:

Boundaries I set:

Problem areas I noticed:

I am grateful for

Reflections

I was good to myself:

Date

Ways I handled conflicts:

Boundaries I set:

Problem areas I noticed:

I am grateful for

Reflections

I was good to myself:

Date

Ways I handled conflicts:

Boundaries I set:

Problem areas I noticed:

I am grateful for

Reflections

Date

I was good to myself:

Ways I handled conflicts:

Boundaries I set:

Problem areas I noticed:

I am grateful for

Reflections

I was good to myself:

Date

Ways I handled conflicts:

Boundaries I set:

Problem areas I noticed:

I am grateful for

Reflections

I was good to myself:

Date

Ways I handled conflicts:

Boundaries I set:

Problem areas I noticed:

I am grateful for

Reflections

I was good to myself:

Date

Ways I handled conflicts:

Boundaries I set:

Problem areas I noticed:

I am grateful for

Reflections

I was good to myself:

Date

Ways I handled conflicts:

Boundaries I set:

Problem areas I noticed:

I am grateful for

Reflections

I was good to myself:

Date

Ways I handled conflicts:

Boundaries I set:

Problem areas I noticed:

I am grateful for

Reflections

I was good to myself:

Date

Ways I handled conflicts:

Boundaries I set:

Problem areas I noticed:

I am grateful for

Reflections

I was good to myself:

Date

Ways I handled conflicts:

Boundaries I set:

Problem areas I noticed:

I am grateful for

Reflections

I was good to myself:

Date

Ways I handled conflicts:

Boundaries I set:

Problem areas I noticed:

I am grateful for

Reflections

I was good to myself:

Date

Ways I handled conflicts:

Boundaries I set:

Problem areas I noticed:

I am grateful for

Reflections

I was good to myself:

Date

Ways I handled conflicts:

Boundaries I set:

Problem areas I noticed:

I am grateful for

Reflections

I was good to myself:

Date

Ways I handled conflicts:

Boundaries I set:

Problem areas I noticed:

I am grateful for

Reflections

I was good to myself:

Boundaries I set:

I am grateful for

Date

Ways I handled conflicts:

Problem areas I noticed:

Reflections

I was good to myself:

Date

Ways I handled conflicts:

Boundaries I set:

Problem areas I noticed:

I am grateful for

Reflections

I was good to myself:

Date

Ways I handled conflicts:

Boundaries I set:

Problem areas I noticed:

I am grateful for

Reflections

I was good to myself:

Date

Ways I handled conflicts:

Boundaries I set:

Problem areas I noticed:

I am grateful for

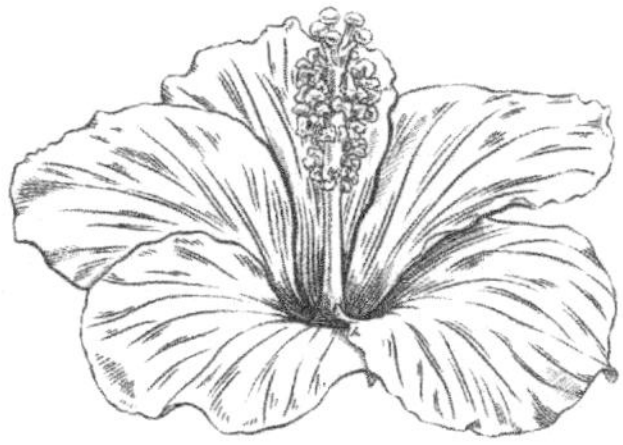

Reflections

I was good to myself:

Date

Ways I handled conflicts:

Boundaries I set:

Problem areas I noticed:

I am grateful for

Reflections

I was good to myself:

Date

Ways I handled conflicts:

Boundaries I set:

Problem areas I noticed:

I am grateful for

Reflections

I was good to myself:

Boundaries I set:

I am grateful for

Date

Ways I handled conflicts:

Problem areas I noticed:

Reflections

I was good to myself:

Date

Ways I handled conflicts:

Boundaries I set:

Problem areas I noticed:

I am grateful for

Reflections

I was good to myself:

Date

Ways I handled conflicts:

Boundaries I set:

Problem areas I noticed:

I am grateful for

Reflections

I was good to myself:

Date

Ways I handled conflicts:

Boundaries I set:

Problem areas I noticed:

I am grateful for

Reflections

I was good to myself:

Date

Ways I handled conflicts:

Boundaries I set:

Problem areas I noticed:

I am grateful for

Reflections

I was good to myself:

Date

Ways I handled conflicts:

Boundaries I set:

Problem areas I noticed:

I am grateful for

Reflections

I was good to myself:

Date

Ways I handled conflicts:

Boundaries I set:

Problem areas I noticed:

I am grateful for

Reflections

I was good to myself:

Date

Ways I handled conflicts:

Boundaries I set:

Problem areas I noticed:

I am grateful for

Reflections

I was good to myself:

Date

Ways I handled conflicts:

Boundaries I set:

Problem areas I noticed:

I am grateful for

Reflections

I was good to myself:

Date

Ways I handled conflicts:

Boundaries I set:

Problem areas I noticed:

I am grateful for

Reflections

I was good to myself:

Boundaries I set:

I am grateful for

Date

Ways I handled conflicts:

Problem areas I noticed:

Reflections

I was good to myself:

Date

Ways I handled conflicts:

Boundaries I set:

Problem areas I noticed:

I am grateful for

Reflections

I was good to myself:

Date

Ways I handled conflicts:

Boundaries I set:

Problem areas I noticed:

I am grateful for

Reflections

I was good to myself:

Date

Ways I handled conflicts:

Boundaries I set:

Problem areas I noticed:

I am grateful for

Reflections

I was good to myself:

Date

Ways I handled conflicts:

Boundaries I set:

Problem areas I noticed:

I am grateful for

Reflections

I was good to myself:

Date

Ways I handled conflicts:

Boundaries I set:

Problem areas I noticed:

I am grateful for

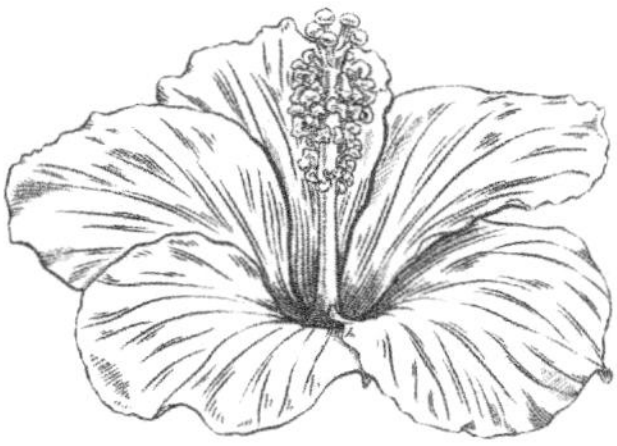

Reflections

I was good to myself:

Date

Ways I handled conflicts:

Boundaries I set:

Problem areas I noticed:

I am grateful for

Reflections

I was good to myself:

Date

Ways I handled conflicts:

Boundaries I set:

Problem areas I noticed:

I am grateful for

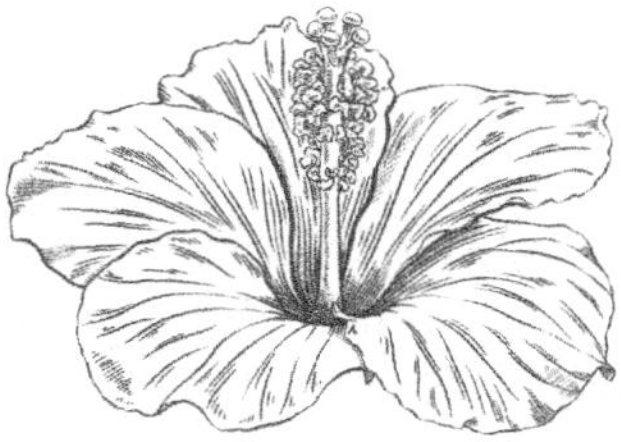

Reflections

I was good to myself:

Boundaries I set:

I am grateful for

Date

Ways I handled conflicts:

Problem areas I noticed:

Reflections

I was good to myself:

Date

Ways I handled conflicts:

Boundaries I set:

Problem areas I noticed:

I am grateful for

Reflections

I was good to myself:

Date

Ways I handled conflicts:

Boundaries I set:

Problem areas I noticed:

I am grateful for

Reflections

I was good to myself:

Boundaries I set:

I am grateful for

Date

Ways I handled conflicts:

Problem areas I noticed:

Reflections

I was good to myself:

Boundaries I set:

I am grateful for

Reflections

Date

Ways I handled conflicts:

Problem areas I noticed:

I was good to myself:

Date

Ways I handled conflicts:

Boundaries I set:

Problem areas I noticed:

I am grateful for

Reflections

I was good to myself:

Boundaries I set:

I am grateful for

Date

Ways I handled conflicts:

Problem areas I noticed:

Reflections

I was good to myself:

Date

Ways I handled conflicts:

Boundaries I set:

Problem areas I noticed:

I am grateful for

Reflections

Date

I was good to myself:

Ways I handled conflicts:

Boundaries I set:

Problem areas I noticed:

I am grateful for

Reflections